The Power Within

Harnessing Motivation to Conquer Challenges and Achieve Greatness

Hadley Tillery

loss due to the information herein, either directly or indirectly. Respective authors own all copyrights not held by the publisher. The information herein is offered for informational purposes solely, and is universal as so. The presentation of the information is without contract or any type of guarantee assurance. The trademarks that are used are without any consent, and the publication of the trademark is without permission or backing by the trademark owner. All trademarks and brands within this book are for clarifying purposes only and are the owned by the owners themselves, not affiliated with this document.

Table of Contents

Chapter 1

Understanding Motivation

The Psychology Behind Motivation

Motivation is an intricate tapestry woven from the threads of human desires, goals, and emotions. It is the driving force that propels individuals to take action, pursue dreams, and overcome obstacles. Understanding the psychology behind motivation unlocks the potential to harness its power effectively. At its core, motivation is the process that initiates, guides, and sustains goal-oriented behaviors. It is the spark that ignites when a person sees a desirable outcome and the fuel that keeps them moving forward to achieve it.

The psychological underpinnings of motivation can be traced to various theories that seek to explain why and how motivation occurs. One of the foundational theories is Maslow's Hierarchy of Needs, which posits that human motivation is driven by the fulfillment of needs, ranging from basic physiological requirements to higher-level self-actualization. According to Maslow, individuals are motivated to fulfill their lower-level needs before progressing to higher ones. This theory highlights the importance of understanding individual needs to comprehend what motivates them uniquely.

Another pivotal concept in motivation psychology is the Self-Determination Theory (SDT), which emphasizes the role of intrinsic and extrinsic motivation. Intrinsic motivation arises from within an individual, driven by personal satisfaction, interest, or enjoyment in the task itself. In contrast, extrinsic motivation is fueled by external rewards or pressures, such as money, praise, or deadlines. SDT suggests that intrinsic motivation is more sustainable and leads to higher satisfaction and performance, as it aligns with an individual's core values and interests. By understanding the balance between intrinsic and extrinsic motivation, individuals and organizations can create environments that foster sustained motivation and engagement.

The Expectancy Theory of Motivation proposes that individuals are motivated by the expected outcome of their actions. It suggests that motivation is a function of three components: expectancy, instrumentality, and valence. Expectancy is the belief that one's effort will lead to successful performance. Instrumentality is the belief that successful performance will result in a desired outcome. Valence is the value an individual places on the outcome. When these components align positively, motivation is enhanced. This theory underscores the importance of setting realistic goals and providing clear pathways to achieve them, thus increasing the likelihood of motivation being sustained.

Emotions play a significant role in shaping motivation. Positive emotions, such as joy, enthusiasm, and hope, can enhance motivation by creating a sense of optimism and possibility. Conversely, negative emotions, such as fear, anxiety, or frustration, can either hinder motivation or, in some cases, act as powerful motivators to avoid undesirable outcomes. Understanding the emotional landscape of motivation allows individuals to harness positive emotions and manage negative ones effectively, thereby creating a balanced motivational drive.

Motivation is also influenced by cognitive processes, including beliefs, attitudes, and perceptions. The concept of self-efficacy, or the belief in one's ability to succeed, is a critical determinant of motivation. High self-efficacy enhances motivation by increasing confidence and persistence, while low self-efficacy can lead to procrastination and avoidance behaviors. Cognitive dissonance, the discomfort experienced when holding conflicting beliefs or attitudes, can also impact motivation. Individuals are motivated to reduce dissonance by changing their beliefs, attitudes, or behaviors to achieve consistency.

The role of goals in motivation cannot be overstated. Goal-setting theory posits that specific, challenging goals enhance motivation and performance more effectively than vague or easy goals. Goals provide direction, focus, and a sense of purpose, channeling motivation towards achieving desired outcomes. However, the nature of the goals set is crucial. Goals that are too rigid or unrealistic can lead to demotivation and burnout, while flexible, attainable goals foster sustained motivation. The process of setting, pursuing, and achieving goals is a dynamic one, requiring regular reflection and adjustment to maintain motivation.

Social and environmental factors also significantly impact motivation. The presence of supportive social networks, positive role models, and encouraging environments can enhance motivation by providing resources, feedback, and reinforcement. Conversely, negative social influences, such as criticism, competition, or lack of support, can diminish motivation. The interplay between individual motivation and social context highlights the importance of creating motivating environments that align with individual needs and values.

Motivation is not a static state but a dynamic process that evolves over time. It can wax and wane in response to changing circumstances, achievements, and setbacks. Building resilience and adaptability is essential to maintaining motivation in the face of challenges. Resilient individuals view setbacks as opportunities for growth and learning, rather than insurmountable obstacles. Cultivating a mindset that embraces change and views failure as a stepping stone to success enhances long-term motivation and perseverance.

Intrinsic vs. Extrinsic Motivation

Motivation is a multifaceted and dynamic force, intricately interwoven into the fabric of human behavior. The distinction between intrinsic and extrinsic motivation provides a lens through which we can better understand the nuances of what drives us. Intrinsic motivation arises from within, fueled by personal satisfaction and interest in the activity itself. Extrinsic motivation, on the other hand, is driven by external factors, such as rewards, recognition, or avoiding negative consequences. Each type of motivation plays a unique role in shaping our actions and decisions, and understanding their interplay can unlock the potential for achieving sustained motivation and fulfillment.

Intrinsic motivation is characterized by a deep sense of engagement and enjoyment in the task at hand. It is the feeling of being "in the zone," where time seems to fly by and the activity itself becomes its own reward. This type of motivation is often found in activities that align with personal passions, interests, or values. For instance, an artist may lose themselves in the process of creating a masterpiece, driven by the joy of expression and creativity, rather than by the prospect of selling the artwork. Intrinsic motivation is associated with higher levels of creativity, persistence, and overall satisfaction, as it taps into the core of what makes an activity meaningful and enjoyable.

The benefits of intrinsic motivation extend beyond personal satisfaction. When individuals are intrinsically motivated, they are more likely to engage in deep learning, take on challenges, and exhibit resilience in the face of setbacks. This type of motivation promotes a sense of autonomy and self-determination, as individuals are guided by their own interests and desires rather than external pressures. Intrinsic motivation is closely linked to a growth mindset, where individuals embrace the process of learning and development for its own sake, rather than for external validation or rewards.

Extrinsic motivation, in contrast, is driven by external factors and influences. It is the motivation to perform a task in order to receive a reward or avoid a negative outcome. Common examples of extrinsic motivators include money, grades, praise, or the fear of punishment. While extrinsic motivation can be effective in certain contexts, such as encouraging individuals to complete tasks or meet deadlines, it often lacks the depth and sustainability of intrinsic motivation. When individuals are motivated primarily by external rewards, they may become dependent on those rewards to maintain their motivation, leading to a decrease in intrinsic interest over time.

The interplay between intrinsic and extrinsic motivation can be complex and context-dependent. In some cases, extrinsic rewards can undermine intrinsic motivation, a phenomenon known as the overjustification effect. When individuals are offered external rewards for activities they already enjoy, their intrinsic motivation may diminish, as the focus shifts from the enjoyment of the activity to the pursuit of the reward. However, extrinsic motivation can also enhance intrinsic motivation when it is used to acknowledge and reinforce an individual's competence or progress, rather than as a controlling mechanism.

Balancing intrinsic and extrinsic motivation is crucial for achieving sustained motivation and success. For individuals and organizations, creating environments that foster intrinsic motivation while strategically leveraging extrinsic motivators can lead to optimal performance and well-being. This balance can be achieved by aligning external rewards with personal values and goals, providing meaningful feedback, and creating opportunities for autonomy and self-expression.

One effective strategy for fostering intrinsic motivation is to create a sense of purpose and meaning in the tasks and activities individuals undertake. When individuals understand how their work aligns with their personal values or contributes to a larger goal, they are more likely to experience intrinsic motivation. For example, a teacher who is motivated by the desire to make a positive impact on students' lives may find intrinsic satisfaction in developing engaging lesson plans and fostering a supportive classroom environment. By focusing on the meaningful aspects of their work, individuals can tap into their intrinsic motivation and maintain their passion and commitment over time.

Providing opportunities for autonomy and self-direction is another key component of fostering intrinsic motivation. When individuals have the freedom to choose how they approach tasks and activities, they are more likely to feel a sense of ownership and investment in their work. This autonomy can lead to greater creativity, problem-solving, and innovation, as individuals explore new ways of achieving their goals.

While extrinsic motivation can be an effective tool for encouraging specific behaviors or outcomes, it is important to use it judiciously and in ways that complement intrinsic motivation. Extrinsic rewards should be used as a form of recognition and encouragement, rather than as a means of controlling behavior. By acknowledging individuals' efforts and achievements, extrinsic rewards can reinforce a sense of competence and progress, enhancing intrinsic motivation in the process.

Motivation Myths and Truths

Motivation is a powerful force, yet it is often shrouded in myths and misconceptions that can obscure its true nature. These myths can hinder personal growth and achievement, leading individuals to adopt ineffective strategies or harbor unrealistic expectations. By unraveling these myths and uncovering the truths behind motivation, one can better harness its potential and achieve sustained success.

One common myth is that motivation is a constant state of being, something that can be permanently achieved and maintained. In reality, motivation is dynamic and fluctuating. It ebbs and flows in response to various internal and external factors, such as mood, environment, stress levels, and life events. Understanding this truth allows individuals to approach motivation with flexibility and adaptability. Rather than expecting to be constantly motivated, it is more effective to develop strategies to reignite motivation during periods of decline. This might involve revisiting one's goals, seeking inspiration from others, or creating new challenges to renew one's sense of purpose.

Another prevalent myth is that motivation is solely dependent on willpower and self-discipline. While these traits are undoubtedly important, they are not the sole determinants of motivation. Motivation is influenced by a myriad of factors, including emotions, cognition, and environment. For instance, a supportive social network, an inspiring work environment, and positive feedback can significantly enhance motivation. Recognizing the interplay of these factors allows individuals to cultivate motivation more holistically, rather than relying solely on sheer willpower.

A widespread misconception is that extrinsic rewards are the most effective motivators. While external incentives such as money, praise, or recognition can drive motivation, they often lack the depth and sustainability of intrinsic motivation. Extrinsic rewards can sometimes undermine intrinsic motivation, leading to a decrease in engagement and satisfaction once the rewards are removed. The truth is that intrinsic motivation, driven by personal interest, passion, and satisfaction, has a more profound and lasting impact. By aligning activities with personal values and interests, individuals can tap into the power of intrinsic motivation and maintain a more enduring drive.

The myth that motivation is the same for everyone can lead to ineffective strategies and frustration. Motivation is highly individualized, varying from person to person based on their unique goals, values, and circumstances. What motivates one person may not necessarily motivate another. Understanding this truth emphasizes the importance of personalized approaches to motivation. Individuals must identify their own sources of inspiration and tailor their motivational strategies accordingly. This could involve setting personal goals, seeking out role models, or creating environments that align with their values.

A common myth is that fear and anxiety are effective motivators. While these emotions can sometimes spur action in the short term, they are rarely sustainable motivators in the long run. Fear-based motivation can lead to stress, burnout, and avoidance behaviors, ultimately hindering performance and well-being. The truth is that positive emotions such as enthusiasm, hope, and curiosity are far more effective in fostering sustained motivation. By cultivating a positive mindset and focusing on the potential benefits and rewards of achieving a goal, individuals can enhance their motivation and maintain their drive over time.

The notion that achieving goals is the ultimate source of motivation is another misconception. While achieving goals can certainly boost motivation, the process of working towards a goal is often more motivating than the outcome itself. The journey towards achieving a goal provides opportunities for growth, learning, and self-discovery, which can be deeply motivating. Embracing the process and finding joy in the journey allows individuals to sustain their motivation, even in the face of setbacks or delays.

Many believe that motivation is something that can be imposed from the outside, such as through motivational speeches or external rewards. While these can provide temporary boosts, true motivation must come from within. It is an internal drive that is cultivated through self-reflection, goal setting, and alignment with personal values. Understanding this truth empowers individuals to take ownership of their motivation, fostering a sense of autonomy and self-determination.

There is also a myth that motivation is only necessary for achieving grand or ambitious goals. In truth, motivation is essential for all aspects of life, from daily tasks to long-term aspirations. It is the driving force behind everything from completing mundane chores to pursuing lifelong dreams. By recognizing the importance of motivation in all areas of life, individuals can develop a more balanced and holistic approach to maintaining their drive and enthusiasm.

Finally, the belief that motivation is a linear process can lead to discouragement when setbacks occur. Motivation is not a straightforward path; it is a journey filled with ups and downs. It is natural to encounter obstacles and experience fluctuations in motivation along the way. The truth is that resilience and adaptability are key components of sustained motivation. By viewing setbacks as opportunities for growth and learning, individuals can maintain their motivation and continue moving forward, even in the face of challenges.

The Role of Emotions in Motivation

Emotions are a fundamental aspect of the human experience, deeply intertwined with our motivations and actions. They serve as powerful catalysts, influencing the decisions we make and the paths we choose to follow. Understanding the role of emotions in motivation provides valuable insights into how we can harness their power to drive us toward our goals and dreams.

Emotions are complex responses to internal and external stimuli, encompassing a wide range of feelings, from joy and excitement to fear and anger. They are intimately connected to our motivations, as they can either propel us forward or hold us back. Positive emotions, such as happiness, enthusiasm, and curiosity, often enhance motivation by creating a sense of optimism and possibility. They encourage us to explore new opportunities, take risks, and persevere in the pursuit of our goals. When we experience joy or excitement about a particular task or project, we are more likely to engage with it wholeheartedly and persist in the face of challenges.

Conversely, negative emotions, such as fear, anxiety, or frustration, can have a complex impact on motivation. In some cases, they may serve as powerful motivators, spurring us to take action to avoid undesirable outcomes or to overcome obstacles. For example, the fear of failure can drive us to work harder and prepare more thoroughly for an exam or presentation. However, when negative emotions become overwhelming or chronic, they can hinder motivation and lead to avoidance behaviors, procrastination, or burnout. Recognizing the dual nature of negative emotions allows us to manage them effectively, using them as a source of motivation when appropriate and mitigating their impact when they become detrimental.

Emotions also play a crucial role in shaping our goals and aspirations. They provide valuable feedback, helping us determine what is important to us and what we truly value. When we experience a strong emotional response to a particular idea or vision, it signals that it holds significance for us, motivating us to pursue it with greater intensity. By tuning into our emotional responses, we can gain clarity about our priorities and align our motivations with our authentic desires and values.

The interplay between emotions and motivation is further complicated by individual differences in emotional regulation and resilience. Some individuals possess a natural ability to manage their emotions effectively, using them to fuel their motivation and drive. Others may struggle with emotional regulation, finding it challenging to harness their emotions in a way that supports their goals. Developing emotional intelligence, the ability to recognize, understand, and manage emotions, is a crucial skill for enhancing motivation. By cultivating emotional intelligence, individuals can learn to navigate their emotional landscape, using positive emotions to bolster motivation and addressing negative emotions in a constructive manner.

Emotional intelligence also involves empathy, the ability to understand and share the feelings of others. Empathy can enhance motivation by fostering a sense of connection and purpose. When we empathize with others, we are motivated to act in ways that benefit them, whether it's through collaborative efforts, acts of kindness, or social advocacy. This sense of purpose and connection can be a powerful motivator, driving us to work towards goals that have a positive impact on the world around us.

The relationship between emotions and motivation is not only internal but also influenced by external factors, such as social interactions and environmental contexts. Positive social interactions, characterized by support, encouragement, and validation, can enhance motivation by boosting positive emotions and fostering a sense of belonging. Conversely, negative social interactions, marked by criticism, rejection, or conflict, can dampen motivation by eliciting negative emotions and eroding self-confidence. Creating a supportive social environment that nurtures positive emotions and reinforces motivation is essential for achieving sustained success.

The physical environment also plays a role in shaping emotions and motivation. A well-designed workspace that promotes comfort, creativity, and focus can enhance positive emotions and motivation, while a cluttered or chaotic environment may lead to stress and distraction. Paying attention to the emotional impact of our surroundings and making adjustments to create a motivating environment can significantly influence our motivation and productivity.

Emotions are not static; they fluctuate in response to changing circumstances, experiences, and perceptions. This dynamic nature of emotions requires us to be adaptable and resilient in our approach to motivation. Building resilience involves developing the ability to bounce back from setbacks and maintain motivation in the face of adversity. It requires cultivating a growth mindset, viewing challenges as opportunities for growth, and embracing change as a natural part of the journey. By building resilience, individuals can maintain their motivation and continue moving forward, even when faced with emotional challenges.

Harnessing the power of emotions in motivation involves a delicate balance between acknowledging and embracing our emotions while maintaining focus and discipline in the pursuit of our goals. It requires self-awareness, the ability to recognize and understand our emotional responses, and self-regulation, the ability to manage those responses in a way that supports our motivation. By developing these skills, individuals can tap into the full potential of their emotions, using them as a source of inspiration and drive.

How Motivation Shapes Our Lives

Motivation, the invisible force that drives us to act, shapes every aspect of our lives. It is interwoven into the fabric of our daily experiences, influencing our choices, behaviors, and goals. By understanding the profound impact motivation has, we can begin to harness its power to create meaningful change and growth.

From the moment we wake up, motivation propels us through a series of decisions and actions. It determines whether we hit the snooze button or leap out of bed, whether we choose a healthy breakfast or opt for convenience. Each decision is a reflection of our underlying motivations, be they health, productivity, or comfort. These seemingly mundane choices accumulate over time, shaping our habits and, ultimately, our lives.

Motivation fuels our ambitions and aspirations, guiding us toward our long-term goals. It is the reason we pursue education, strive for career advancement, and work tirelessly to achieve personal milestones. Consider the student who sacrifices weekends to study for exams, motivated by the desire to excel academically and secure a promising future. Or the entrepreneur who risks financial security to launch a startup, driven by the vision of creating something impactful. In both cases, motivation acts as the catalyst that transforms dreams into reality.

The role of motivation extends beyond individual pursuits, influencing our relationships and interactions with others. It motivates us to seek connection, build meaningful bonds, and support those we care about. Motivation can drive acts of kindness, empathy, and generosity, enriching our social networks and fostering a sense of belonging. Conversely, a lack of motivation can lead to isolation and disconnection, underscoring its importance in maintaining healthy, fulfilling relationships.

Motivation also plays a critical role in our resilience and ability to overcome challenges. Life is replete with obstacles and setbacks that test our resolve and determination. Motivation provides the strength to persevere in the face of adversity, to adapt and find new solutions when confronted with difficulties. It is the engine that powers resilience, enabling individuals to bounce back stronger and more determined than before. This ability to adapt and grow is a testament to the transformative power of motivation.

Moreover, motivation shapes our self-perception and identity. It influences the way we view ourselves, our capabilities, and our potential. When motivated, we are more likely to set ambitious goals, embrace challenges, and push beyond our comfort zones. This, in turn, fosters a positive self-image and a sense of accomplishment. Conversely, a lack of motivation can lead to self-doubt, limiting beliefs, and a reluctance to pursue opportunities for growth. By nurturing motivation, we cultivate a mindset that is open to new experiences and confident in its own potential.

The impact of motivation is also evident in the workplace, where it drives productivity, innovation, and job satisfaction. Motivated employees are more engaged, committed, and willing to go the extra mile to achieve organizational goals. They bring creativity and enthusiasm to their roles, contributing to a positive work environment and a culture of excellence. Employers who understand the importance of motivation invest in creating conditions that foster it, such as providing opportunities for skill development, recognizing achievements, and promoting work-life balance.

In the realm of personal development, motivation serves as the foundation for self-improvement and lifelong learning. It inspires individuals to acquire new skills, expand their knowledge, and pursue passions that enrich their lives. Whether it's learning a new language, mastering a musical instrument, or adopting a healthier lifestyle, motivation is the driving force that turns intentions into actions. It provides the focus and commitment needed to persist in the face of challenges and setbacks, ultimately leading to personal growth and fulfillment.

The influence of motivation extends to societal and cultural change. Throughout history, motivated individuals have been the catalysts for social movements, scientific discoveries, and artistic revolutions. Their passion and determination have led to groundbreaking advancements and transformative shifts that have shaped the course of human history. From civil rights activists to visionary leaders, these individuals demonstrate the power of motivation to effect positive change on a global scale.

To harness the power of motivation effectively, it is essential to cultivate a mindset that is open to exploration and growth. This involves setting clear, meaningful goals that resonate with our values and aspirations. By aligning our actions with our intrinsic motivations, we create a sense of purpose and direction that fuels sustained effort and commitment. Additionally, surrounding ourselves with supportive environments and individuals who share our values can reinforce motivation and provide encouragement when needed.

It is also important to recognize the dynamic nature of motivation and be adaptable in our approach.

Motivation is not a constant; it fluctuates in response to changes in circumstances, emotions, and priorities. By being attuned to these shifts, we can adjust our strategies and goals to maintain motivation and momentum. This adaptability allows us to navigate life's complexities with resilience and determination, ensuring that motivation continues to shape our lives in positive and meaningful ways.

Chapter 2

Identifying Your Inner Drive

Discovering Your Passion

Passion is the lifeblood of motivation, a powerful force that imbues our lives with meaning and direction. It is the spark that ignites our enthusiasm, driving us to pursue our dreams with unwavering determination. Yet, for many, discovering one's passion can feel like an elusive quest, obscured by the demands and distractions of daily life. By embarking on a journey of self-discovery and introspection, we can uncover the passions that lie within, paving the way for a more fulfilling and purpose-driven existence.

The first step in discovering your passion is to engage in honest self-reflection. This involves setting aside time to consider your interests, values, and experiences, asking yourself what truly excites and inspires you. Think back to moments when you felt most alive and engaged, when time seemed to fly by as you immersed yourself in an activity. These moments can provide valuable clues to your passions, revealing the activities and pursuits that resonate with your inner self.

It is important to approach this process with an open mind, free from preconceived notions or external expectations. Passion is deeply personal, and what resonates with one person may not hold the same significance for another. Avoid the temptation to compare your interests to those of others or to pursue a path simply because it is deemed prestigious or lucrative. Authentic passion is born from within, rooted in your unique identity and aspirations.

Exploration is a key component in the journey to discovering your passion. This involves stepping outside your comfort zone, trying new activities, and embracing a spirit of curiosity and adventure. Attend workshops, enroll in classes, or volunteer for projects that pique your interest, even if they seem unrelated to your current pursuits. By exposing yourself to diverse experiences, you broaden your horizons and open the door to new possibilities. You may be surprised by what captures your imagination and ignites your enthusiasm.

While exploring new interests, pay attention to the emotions and sensations they evoke. Passion is often accompanied by a sense of joy, excitement, and fulfillment, a feeling of being "in the zone" where time seems to disappear. It is a state of flow, where you are fully immersed and engaged in the activity. When you encounter this feeling, take note, as it may indicate a potential passion worth pursuing further.

It is also helpful to examine the intersection of your skills and interests. Consider the activities that come naturally to you, those in which you excel with ease and confidence. Passion often aligns with our innate talents and abilities, allowing us to express ourselves authentically and effortlessly. By identifying the areas where your skills and interests converge, you can gain insight into potential passions that are both fulfilling and rewarding.

As you navigate the path to discovering your passion, be mindful of the obstacles that may arise. Fear of failure, self-doubt, and societal pressures can deter you from pursuing your true interests. Recognize these barriers for what they are—temporary challenges that can be overcome with perseverance and resilience. Embrace a growth mindset, viewing setbacks as opportunities for learning and growth. By cultivating self-compassion and patience, you create a supportive environment for your passion to flourish.

Networking and connecting with others who share your interests can also facilitate the discovery of your passion. Engage with communities, clubs, or online forums related to your areas of interest, and seek out mentors or role models who inspire you. These connections can provide valuable insights, encouragement, and opportunities to deepen your engagement with your passion. Sharing your experiences with like-minded individuals fosters a sense of belonging and reinforces your commitment to your pursuits.

It is important to acknowledge that discovering your passion is not always a linear or straightforward process. It may involve detours, experimentation, and periods of uncertainty. Be open to the evolution of your interests, recognizing that passion can change and develop over time. What excites you today may differ from what inspires you in the future, and that is perfectly natural. Embrace the journey of discovery with an open heart and mind, allowing your passion to unfold organically.

Once you have identified a passion, nurture it by integrating it into your daily life. Set aside time to engage in activities related to your passion, whether through hobbies, projects, or professional pursuits. Prioritize your passion by creating routines or rituals that honor your commitment to it. By making your passion a consistent part of your life, you reinforce its importance and create a sense of purpose and fulfillment.

Balancing passion with practicality is essential for sustaining motivation and well-being. While it is important to pursue your passions, it is equally important to consider the practical aspects of your life, such as financial stability and personal responsibilities. Strive for a balance that allows you to honor your passion while meeting your essential needs. This may involve creative solutions, such as pursuing your passion part-time, integrating it into your current career, or gradually transitioning to a new path.

Setting Meaningful Goals

Goals serve as the compass guiding us through the myriad possibilities life presents, offering a sense of direction and purpose in our personal and professional journeys. Setting meaningful goals is an essential skill that enables us to focus our efforts, measure our progress, and ultimately achieve a sense of accomplishment. However, the art of goal-setting extends beyond simply identifying what we want to achieve; it requires thoughtful deliberation and strategic planning to ensure that our goals align with our values and aspirations.

A meaningful goal begins with a clear vision of what you hope to achieve. This vision must be specific, detailed, and vivid, much like a mental blueprint that guides you as you progress. A vague or abstract goal can lead to confusion and a lack of motivation. For instance, rather than setting a goal to "be healthier," consider specifying what that entails for you, such as "exercise for 30 minutes daily" or "eat five servings of fruits and vegetables each day." Specificity provides clarity, making the goal more tangible and actionable.

In addition to specificity, meaningful goals should be measurable. This involves establishing criteria for tracking progress and determining when the goal has been achieved. Measurable goals allow you to quantify your progress, providing valuable feedback and motivation as you move forward. For example, if your goal is to write a novel, setting a target word count per day or week creates a measurable framework to track your writing progress. This quantitative approach helps maintain momentum and keeps you accountable to your objectives.

Aligning your goals with your core values and passions is crucial for ensuring their meaningfulness. Goals that resonate with your values and passions are inherently motivating, as they reflect your authentic desires and aspirations. Take time to reflect on what truly matters to you, considering your long-term vision and the impact you want to make in your life and the lives of others. By aligning your goals with your values, you create a sense of purpose and fulfillment that fuels your motivation and commitment.

While ambitious goals can be inspiring, it is essential to balance ambition with realism. Setting goals that are too far beyond your current capabilities can lead to frustration and discouragement, while goals that are too easily attainable may lack the challenge needed to inspire growth. Strive for a balance that stretches your abilities while remaining within the realm of possibility. Consider breaking larger goals into smaller, manageable milestones, each serving as a stepping stone towards the ultimate objective. This approach not only makes the goal more achievable but also provides regular opportunities for celebration and reflection on your progress.

Time-bound goals are another key element of effective goal-setting. Establishing deadlines creates a sense of urgency and encourages consistent effort towards the goal. Without a timeframe, goals can become open-ended, leading to procrastination and a lack of focus. Determine a realistic timeline for achieving your goal, taking into account any external factors or dependencies that may influence your progress. Be open to adjusting your timeline as needed, allowing for flexibility in response to unforeseen challenges or opportunities.

An essential component of meaningful goal-setting is the ability to anticipate and address potential obstacles. Challenges are an inevitable part of any journey, and preparing for them can prevent setbacks from derailing your progress. Consider potential barriers to achieving your goal and develop strategies for overcoming them. This may involve acquiring new skills, seeking support from others, or adjusting your approach as needed. By proactively addressing obstacles, you build resilience and confidence in your ability to navigate the path ahead.

Accountability is a powerful motivator in achieving goals, providing an external source of encouragement and support. Sharing your goals with others, whether through a formal accountability partner or an informal support network, increases your commitment and motivation. Regular check-ins with your accountability partner can provide valuable feedback, encouragement, and guidance as you work towards your goal. Additionally, consider documenting your progress through a journal or digital platform, creating a record of your journey that you can reflect upon and learn from.

Reflection and adjustment are integral to the goal-setting process, allowing you to assess your progress and make any necessary changes to your approach. Regularly evaluate your progress towards your goal, considering what is working well and what may need adjustment. Be open to adapting your strategies or even redefining your goals as your circumstances and priorities evolve. This iterative process of reflection and adjustment ensures that your goals remain relevant and meaningful, aligned with your evolving vision and values.

Celebrating achievements, both big and small, is an important aspect of maintaining motivation and momentum. Recognize and reward yourself for reaching milestones and making progress towards your goal. Celebrations can take many forms, from personal acknowledgments to sharing your success with others. These moments of celebration serve as reminders of your progress and the value of your efforts, reinforcing your commitment and enthusiasm for the journey ahead.

Recognizing What Truly Inspires You

Inspiration is a powerful catalyst for creativity, innovation, and personal growth. It is the spark that ignites our passions, propelling us to explore new horizons and embrace our potential. However, recognizing what truly inspires us can be an elusive endeavor, often clouded by external influences and societal expectations. By embarking on a journey of introspection and exploration, we can uncover the sources of inspiration that resonate most deeply with our authentic selves.

To begin the process of recognizing what truly inspires you, it's essential to engage in self-reflection. This involves delving into your past experiences and identifying moments when you felt most alive and engaged. Consider times when you were filled with excitement, curiosity, or a sense of wonder. These moments, however fleeting, offer valuable insights into the activities, environments, and ideas that inspire you. Reflecting on these experiences can help you identify patterns and themes that point to your true sources of inspiration.

Journaling can be a powerful tool for self-reflection, providing a space to document your thoughts, feelings, and observations. Set aside time each day to write about your experiences, focusing on what energizes and excites you. Pay attention to the stories, people, and events that capture your imagination and stir your emotions. Over time, you may begin to notice recurring motifs that reveal your unique sources of inspiration.

Exploration and experimentation are key components of the journey to recognizing what inspires you. Inspiration often lies outside the confines of our daily routines, waiting to be discovered through new experiences and perspectives. Embrace a spirit of curiosity and openness, seeking out opportunities to explore diverse interests and activities. Attend lectures, visit art galleries, read books on unfamiliar topics, or engage in conversations with people from different backgrounds. These experiences can expand your horizons and introduce you to new ideas that resonate deeply with your core values and passions.

While exploring new interests, pay attention to the emotions and sensations they evoke. Inspiration is often accompanied by a sense of excitement, wonder, and possibility. It is a feeling of being "in the zone," where time seems to stand still and your mind is fully engaged. When you encounter this state, take note, as it may indicate a potential source of inspiration worth pursuing further.

Recognizing what truly inspires you also involves examining the intersection of your skills, interests, and values. Consider the activities that come naturally to you, those in which you excel with ease and confidence. Inspiration often aligns with our innate talents and abilities, allowing us to express ourselves authentically and effortlessly. By identifying the areas where your skills, interests, and values converge, you can gain insight into potential sources of inspiration that are both fulfilling and rewarding.

It's important to be mindful of external influences that may obscure your true sources of inspiration. Societal expectations, cultural norms, and the opinions of others can create pressure to conform to certain paths or ideals. To recognize what truly inspires you, strive to separate your own desires from those imposed by others. This may require setting boundaries, practicing self-compassion, and cultivating a strong sense of self-awareness. By doing so, you create space to explore your authentic interests and passions, free from external constraints.

Connecting with others who share your interests can also facilitate the recognition of your true sources of inspiration. Engage with communities, clubs, or online forums related to your areas of interest, and seek out mentors or role models who inspire you. These connections can provide valuable insights, encouragement, and opportunities to deepen your engagement with your inspiration. Sharing your experiences with like-minded individuals fosters a sense of belonging and reinforces your commitment to your pursuits.

It's essential to acknowledge that recognizing what truly inspires you is not always a linear or straightforward process. It may involve detours, experimentation, and periods of uncertainty. Be open to the evolution of your interests, recognizing that inspiration can change and develop over time. What inspires you today may differ from what inspires you in the future, and that is perfectly natural. Embrace the journey of discovery with an open heart and mind, allowing your sources of inspiration to unfold organically.

Once you have identified a source of inspiration, nurture it by integrating it into your daily life. Set aside time to engage in activities related to your inspiration, whether through hobbies, projects, or professional pursuits. Prioritize your inspiration by creating routines or rituals that honor your commitment to it. By making your inspiration a consistent part of your life, you reinforce its importance and create a sense of purpose and fulfillment.

Balancing inspiration with practicality is essential for sustaining motivation and well-being. While it is important to pursue what inspires you, it is equally important to consider the practical aspects of your life, such as financial stability and personal responsibilities. Strive for a balance that allows you to honor your inspiration while meeting your essential needs. This may involve creative solutions, such as pursuing your inspiration part-time, integrating it into your current career, or gradually transitioning to a new path.

The Importance of Self-Reflection

Self-reflection, the practice of examining one's thoughts, feelings, and actions, serves as a cornerstone for personal growth and self-awareness. It is a powerful tool that allows individuals to gain insight into their inner world, fostering a deeper understanding of their motivations, values, and aspirations. In a fast-paced world that often prioritizes external achievements over internal development, self-reflection offers a much-needed pause, providing clarity and direction in the journey of life.

The importance of self-reflection lies in its ability to cultivate self-awareness, a foundational element of emotional intelligence. By taking the time to reflect on our experiences, we become more attuned to our emotions, recognizing patterns and triggers that influence our behavior. This heightened awareness enables us to respond to situations with greater mindfulness and intention, reducing impulsivity and enhancing our ability to navigate complex interpersonal dynamics.

Through self-reflection, we gain valuable insights into our strengths and weaknesses, empowering us to make informed decisions about our personal and professional lives. By acknowledging our strengths, we can leverage them to achieve our goals and contribute meaningfully to our communities. Conversely, recognizing our weaknesses provides an opportunity for growth and development, allowing us to address areas that may hinder our progress or impact our relationships. This process of self-discovery fosters resilience, adaptability, and a growth mindset, equipping us with the tools needed to thrive in an ever-changing world.

Self-reflection also plays a crucial role in aligning our actions with our values and goals. In the hustle and bustle of daily life, it is easy to become disconnected from our true desires and priorities, leading to feelings of dissatisfaction and discontent. By regularly engaging in self-reflection, we can assess whether our actions align with our core values and long-term objectives, making adjustments as needed to ensure that we are living authentically and purposefully. This alignment creates a sense of coherence and fulfillment, enhancing our overall well-being and satisfaction with life.

Moreover, self-reflection provides an opportunity to learn from past experiences, transforming setbacks and failures into valuable lessons. By examining the factors that contributed to a particular outcome, we can identify areas for improvement and develop strategies to avoid similar pitfalls in the future. This reflective practice shifts our perspective from one of self-criticism to one of self-compassion and growth, fostering a positive and constructive relationship with ourselves.

To incorporate self-reflection into daily life, it is important to establish a routine that encourages consistent practice. Setting aside dedicated time for reflection, whether through journaling, meditation, or quiet contemplation, creates a structured environment for introspection. Journaling, in particular, is an effective method for capturing thoughts and emotions, allowing us to track our progress and gain insight into recurring themes and patterns. Writing about our experiences can also serve as a cathartic release, providing clarity and perspective on complex emotions and situations.

Mindfulness meditation is another valuable practice that encourages self-reflection by fostering present-moment awareness. By focusing on the breath and observing thoughts and emotions without judgment, mindfulness meditation cultivates a sense of detachment and clarity, allowing us to explore our inner world with curiosity and openness. This practice enhances our ability to remain present and attentive, reducing stress and promoting emotional regulation.

While self-reflection is a deeply personal practice, seeking feedback from others can provide valuable external perspectives that enhance our understanding of ourselves. Engaging in open and honest conversations with trusted friends, family members, or mentors can offer insights into our blind spots and areas for growth. By approaching feedback with an open mind and a willingness to learn, we can gain a more comprehensive understanding of how our actions and behaviors impact those around us.

It is important to approach self-reflection with a sense of curiosity and compassion, avoiding self-judgment or criticism. The goal of self-reflection is not to dwell on perceived shortcomings or mistakes but to cultivate a deeper understanding of ourselves and our experiences. By embracing a growth-oriented mindset, we can view challenges and setbacks as opportunities for learning and development, fostering resilience and self-compassion in the face of adversity.

Incorporating self-reflection into our lives requires a commitment to ongoing growth and self-improvement. As we navigate the complexities of life, our values, goals, and priorities may evolve, necessitating regular reflection and reassessment. By making self-reflection a consistent practice, we can remain attuned to our inner world, ensuring that our actions and decisions align with our evolving vision for our lives.

Aligning Values with Ambitions

Aligning values with ambitions is a delicate dance, a harmonious blend of what we hold dear and what we strive to achieve. This alignment serves as a guiding star, ensuring that the pursuit of our goals remains true to our core beliefs and principles. When our ambitions resonate with our values, we are more likely to experience a sense of fulfillment, satisfaction, and authenticity in our lives. However, achieving this alignment requires introspection, clarity, and deliberate action.

To begin this journey, it is essential to clearly define both your values and ambitions. Values are the fundamental beliefs that shape our decisions and behaviors, such as integrity, compassion, creativity, or justice. They serve as the moral compass that guides us through life's challenges and opportunities. Ambitions, on the other hand, are the aspirations and goals we strive to achieve, whether in our personal, professional, or social lives. By identifying and articulating these elements, we lay the groundwork for creating a life that is both meaningful and purpose-driven.

Reflecting on your core values involves an honest examination of what truly matters to you. Take the time to consider moments when you felt aligned and authentic, when your actions mirrored your beliefs and principles. These moments offer valuable insights into the values that underpin your identity. Journaling can be a helpful tool in this process, allowing you to document your reflections and gain deeper clarity on your values. As you explore these reflections, look for recurring themes and patterns that highlight your most cherished beliefs.

Once you have a clear understanding of your values, turn your attention to your ambitions. Consider the goals and aspirations that fuel your passion and drive. What do you hope to achieve, and why? Delve into the motivations behind your ambitions, examining whether they stem from genuine desires or external pressures. This introspection helps ensure that your ambitions are rooted in authenticity rather than societal expectations or fleeting trends.

With a clear picture of your values and ambitions, assess the alignment between the two. Evaluate whether your current goals reflect your core beliefs and whether your actions are consistent with your values. This assessment may reveal areas of misalignment, where your ambitions may be at odds with your values. For instance, you may aspire to achieve career success but find that the means of achieving it compromise your integrity or personal relationships. Recognizing these discrepancies is the first step in realigning your path to ensure that your pursuits honor your values.

Bridging the gap between values and ambitions often involves adjusting your goals or redefining your approach to achieving them. This may require prioritizing certain values over others, making sacrifices, or exploring alternative paths. For example, if environmental sustainability is a core value, you may choose to pursue a career in renewable energy or adopt eco-friendly practices in your daily life. By aligning your ambitions with your values, you create a sense of coherence and integrity, fostering a deep sense of purpose and fulfillment.

It is important to approach this process with flexibility and an open mind. Values and ambitions are not static; they evolve over time as we gain new experiences and insights. Be open to revisiting and re-evaluating your values and goals, allowing for growth and change. This adaptability ensures that your life's path remains aligned with your evolving vision, keeping you true to your authentic self.

Seeking feedback from trusted individuals can provide valuable perspectives on the alignment of your values and ambitions. Engaging in open conversations with friends, family, mentors, or colleagues can offer insights into how your actions and goals are perceived by others. This external feedback can serve as a mirror, reflecting areas where you may be blind to misalignments or opportunities for growth. Approach feedback with an open heart, embracing it as a tool for self-improvement and alignment.

Incorporating practices that reinforce your values can strengthen the alignment with your ambitions. This may involve setting intentions, creating rituals, or engaging in activities that celebrate your core beliefs. For instance, if community service is a value, volunteering regularly can reinforce this commitment and integrate it into your daily life. These practices serve as reminders of what you hold dear, keeping your values at the forefront of your mind as you pursue your ambitions.

As you navigate the complexities of aligning values with ambitions, remember the importance of self-compassion and patience. This journey is not without challenges, and it is natural to encounter setbacks or moments of doubt. Embrace these experiences as opportunities for learning and growth, recognizing that the path to alignment is a continuous exploration rather than a fixed destination.

Chapter 3

Building a Motivational Mindset

Cultivating a Growth Mindset

Cultivating a growth mindset is an empowering journey that transforms how we perceive challenges, failures, and opportunities. It is the belief that our abilities and intelligence can be developed through dedication, effort, and perseverance. This mindset stands in contrast to a fixed mindset, where individuals believe their talents and intelligence are static traits that cannot be changed. By embracing a growth mindset, we unlock our potential, allowing us to approach life's hurdles with resilience, curiosity, and a willingness to learn.

The concept of a growth mindset was popularized by psychologist Carol Dweck, whose research demonstrated the profound impact that our beliefs about ourselves have on our success and happiness. Individuals with a growth mindset view challenges as opportunities for growth, seeing effort as the pathway to mastery. They embrace feedback, learn from criticism, and are inspired by the success of others. In contrast, those with a fixed mindset may avoid challenges, give up easily, and feel threatened by the accomplishments of peers.

To begin cultivating a growth mindset, it is essential to become aware of your current beliefs about your abilities. Start by observing your self-talk and internal dialogue. Do you find yourself saying, "I'm just not good at this" or "I can't do it"? These statements may indicate a fixed mindset at play. By becoming conscious of these thoughts, you can begin to challenge and reframe them. Replace limiting beliefs with growth-oriented affirmations, such as "I am capable of learning this" or "With practice, I can improve."

One effective strategy for fostering a growth mindset is to embrace the power of "yet." This simple word can transform the way we perceive our abilities and progress. Instead of saying, "I can't solve this problem," try saying, "I can't solve this problem yet." The addition of "yet" introduces the possibility of growth and improvement, reinforcing the belief that skills and intelligence are not fixed but can be developed over time.

Reframing challenges as opportunities for growth is another crucial aspect of cultivating a growth mindset. Instead of viewing obstacles as insurmountable barriers, approach them as puzzles to solve or adventures to embark upon. This shift in perspective encourages experimentation, creativity, and problem-solving, fostering a sense of curiosity and excitement about learning. By focusing on the process rather than the outcome, you can reduce the fear of failure and embrace the learning opportunities that challenges present.

Feedback is a valuable tool for growth, yet it is often met with resistance or defensiveness. To cultivate a growth mindset, it is important to view feedback as a gift—a chance to gain insight and improve. Approach feedback with an open mind, seeking to understand and learn from it, even if it is difficult to hear. Constructive criticism can illuminate blind spots and areas for development, guiding you on your path to growth. Remember that feedback is not a reflection of your worth but an opportunity for growth and self-improvement.

Effort is central to the growth mindset, as it is seen as the pathway to mastery and success. Embrace the power of effort by setting goals that challenge you and require persistence and dedication. Recognize that effort is not a sign of inadequacy but a testament to your commitment to learning and growth. Celebrate the hard work and perseverance you invest in your pursuits, valuing the journey as much as the destination.

Learning from failure is a hallmark of the growth mindset, as it transforms setbacks into stepping stones for success. When faced with failure, resist the urge to view it as a reflection of your abilities. Instead, analyze the experience, identifying what went wrong and how you can improve in the future. This reflective practice allows you to extract valuable lessons from failure, turning it into a powerful catalyst for growth and innovation. By viewing failure as an essential part of the learning process, you can approach challenges with courage and resilience.

To strengthen your growth mindset, surround yourself with individuals who embody and encourage this perspective. Seek out mentors, friends, and colleagues who inspire you with their dedication to learning and growth. Engage in conversations that challenge your thinking and expose you to new ideas and perspectives. By immersing yourself in a growth-oriented environment, you reinforce your own commitment to cultivating this mindset.

Cultivating a growth mindset is not a one-time endeavor but an ongoing journey that requires practice and intentionality. It invites us to embrace the unknown, take risks, and step outside our comfort zones. By committing to this path, we open ourselves to a world of possibilities, unleashing our potential and expanding our horizons. As we navigate the complexities of life, a growth mindset empowers us to approach each experience with curiosity, resilience, and an unwavering belief in our capacity to learn and grow.

Overcoming Self-Doubt and Fear

The journey to self-discovery and achievement is often riddled with obstacles, none more insidious than self-doubt and fear. These internal adversaries can cripple ambition, stifle creativity, and inhibit progress. However, by understanding the roots of these feelings and employing strategies to overcome them, one can transform self-doubt and fear into powerful catalysts for growth and resilience.

Self-doubt often arises from a lack of confidence in one's abilities, fueled by past experiences, societal pressures, or internalized criticism. It whispers that you are not good enough, capable enough, or deserving of success. Fear, closely intertwined with self-doubt, manifests as a protective mechanism, warning us of potential failure or rejection. These emotions are natural, but when left unchecked, they can become paralyzing, preventing us from pursuing our goals and dreams.

To overcome self-doubt, it is crucial to challenge the negative narratives that fuel it. Begin by identifying the specific thoughts that undermine your confidence, such as "I'm not talented enough" or "I'll never succeed." Acknowledge these thoughts without judgment and examine their validity. Are they based on facts, or are they assumptions and exaggerations? By questioning the accuracy of these beliefs, you can begin to dismantle their power over you.

One effective technique for countering self-doubt is to reframe negative thoughts into positive affirmations. Instead of focusing on what you lack, emphasize your strengths and potential. For example, replace "I can't handle this" with "I am capable of learning and growing through this experience." Positive affirmations, when practiced consistently, can help rewire your mindset, fostering a sense of self-assurance and empowerment.

Building self-confidence is another essential step in overcoming self-doubt. Confidence is not an innate trait but a skill that can be developed through practice and perseverance. Set small, achievable goals that allow you to experience success and build momentum. Celebrate each accomplishment, no matter how minor, as evidence of your abilities and potential. Over time, these successes accumulate, bolstering your confidence and reinforcing your belief in yourself.

Fear, while often perceived as an obstacle, can be reframed as a guide to personal growth. Rather than avoiding fear, lean into it and explore its origins. What is the underlying concern that fear is trying to protect you from? By understanding the root of your fear, you can address it with clarity and intention. For instance, if fear of failure is holding you back, consider what failure truly means to you and how you can redefine it as a learning opportunity rather than a defeat.

Visualization is a powerful tool for overcoming fear, allowing you to mentally rehearse success and build confidence in your abilities. Visualize yourself navigating challenges with ease, achieving your goals, and embracing new experiences. This mental imagery can help desensitize you to fear, making it less daunting and more manageable. As you practice visualization, focus on the emotions and sensations of success, reinforcing your belief in your capacity to overcome obstacles.

Another strategy for confronting fear is to take incremental steps outside your comfort zone. Start with small, manageable challenges that push your boundaries without overwhelming you. Each step beyond your comfort zone expands your capabilities and resilience, gradually reducing the power of fear. As you become more comfortable with discomfort, you build the courage to tackle larger challenges and pursue your ambitions with confidence.

Seeking support from others is a valuable resource in the battle against self-doubt and fear. Share your feelings and experiences with trusted friends, family members, or mentors who can offer encouragement and perspective. Their insights can illuminate blind spots and provide reassurance that you are not alone in your struggles. Additionally, consider seeking professional support from a therapist or coach who can guide you in developing strategies to manage self-doubt and fear effectively.

Practicing self-compassion is an essential component of overcoming self-doubt and fear. Treat yourself with the same kindness and understanding you would offer a friend facing similar challenges. Acknowledge that everyone experiences self-doubt and fear at times and that these emotions do not define your worth or potential. By embracing self-compassion, you create a nurturing environment for growth and resilience, allowing you to navigate challenges with grace and confidence.

Mindfulness and meditation can also play a significant role in managing self-doubt and fear. These practices cultivate present-moment awareness, allowing you to observe your thoughts and emotions without judgment. By developing mindfulness, you can recognize when self-doubt and fear arise, creating space to respond intentionally rather than react impulsively. Meditation, in particular, can help calm the mind and reduce anxiety, providing a sense of balance and clarity in the face of uncertainty.

Developing Resilience and Grit

In life's unpredictable journey, resilience and grit emerge as powerful allies, equipping us to withstand adversity and pursue our goals with unwavering determination. These qualities are not innate traits but skills that can be cultivated and honed through intentional practice and perseverance. Developing resilience and grit empowers individuals to face challenges head-on, adapt to setbacks, and maintain focus on long-term aspirations, transforming obstacles into stepping stones for growth and achievement.

Resilience, at its core, is the ability to recover from setbacks, adapt to change, and keep moving forward in the face of adversity. It is the mental fortitude that enables individuals to navigate life's inevitable ups and downs with grace and composure. Grit, on the other hand, is the steadfast determination to pursue long-term goals with passion and perseverance, even when progress seems slow or difficult. Together, these qualities form a formidable foundation for personal and professional success.

To develop resilience, it is essential to cultivate a positive mindset that embraces challenges as opportunities for growth. Begin by reframing setbacks and failures as valuable learning experiences rather than insurmountable obstacles. This shift in perspective encourages a proactive approach to problem-solving, fostering creativity and adaptability. By viewing challenges through a lens of curiosity and openness, you can uncover new possibilities and solutions that may have otherwise gone unnoticed.

Building a strong support network is another crucial aspect of resilience. Surround yourself with individuals who uplift and encourage you, providing a safe space for sharing your experiences and emotions. Trusted friends, family members, and mentors can offer guidance, perspective, and reassurance during difficult times, reminding you that you are not alone in your struggles. Engaging with supportive communities fosters a sense of belonging and connection, reinforcing your ability to bounce back from adversity.

Practicing self-care is vital for nurturing resilience, as it ensures that your physical, emotional, and mental well-being are prioritized. Regular exercise, a balanced diet, adequate sleep, and mindfulness practices can help manage stress and enhance your overall resilience. By taking care of yourself, you build a strong foundation from which to face challenges and recover from setbacks. Self-care also includes setting boundaries and saying no when necessary, preserving your energy and resources for what truly matters.

Grit, characterized by unwavering commitment to long-term goals, requires a clear vision of what you wish to achieve. Start by setting meaningful and specific goals that resonate with your values and passions. Break these goals into smaller, manageable steps, creating a roadmap that guides your progress. This approach not only makes your aspirations more attainable but also provides opportunities for celebrating incremental achievements, reinforcing your motivation and persistence.

Perseverance, the hallmark of grit, is cultivated through consistent effort and dedication. Embrace the power of routine by establishing habits that support your goals and aspirations. Whether it's dedicating time each day to practice a skill, setting aside moments for reflection, or maintaining a journal of your progress, these routines create a sense of structure and accountability. By committing to regular practice, you develop discipline and tenacity, enabling you to stay the course even when faced with obstacles.

Emotional regulation is a key component of both resilience and grit, as it allows individuals to manage their emotions effectively and maintain focus on their goals. Practice techniques such as mindfulness meditation, deep breathing, or visualization to calm your mind and regulate your emotions. These practices enhance your ability to respond to stress with clarity and composure, preventing emotional reactions from derailing your progress. By cultivating emotional intelligence, you strengthen your capacity to navigate challenges with resilience and determination.

Learning from setbacks is an integral part of developing resilience and grit. When faced with failure or disappointment, resist the urge to view it as a reflection of your worth or abilities. Instead, analyze the experience objectively, identifying the factors that contributed to the outcome and the lessons you can extract from it. This reflective practice transforms setbacks into valuable opportunities for growth and self-improvement, reinforcing your commitment to your goals.

Flexibility and adaptability are essential qualities for maintaining resilience and grit in the face of changing circumstances. Be open to adjusting your approach, exploring alternative paths, and embracing new perspectives. By remaining flexible, you can pivot when necessary, ensuring that your strategies align with the evolving landscape and your long-term vision. This adaptability enhances your resilience, enabling you to thrive in dynamic environments and maintain focus on your goals.

Ultimately, developing resilience and grit is a journey of self-discovery and empowerment. It requires a commitment to growth, a willingness to embrace challenges, and an unwavering belief in your capacity to overcome obstacles. By cultivating these qualities, you equip yourself with the tools needed to navigate life's complexities with confidence and determination, creating a life that is rich in purpose and fulfillment.

Embracing Change and Adaptability

Change is the only constant, a force that shapes our lives in ways both expected and surprising. Embracing change and cultivating adaptability are essential skills in navigating the complexities of both personal and professional landscapes. They empower individuals to respond to new circumstances with agility and creativity, transforming potential disruptions into opportunities for growth and innovation.

Understanding the nature of change begins with recognizing its inevitability. Whether prompted by external events or internal shifts, change is a natural part of the human experience. It often arrives uninvited, challenging our routines, beliefs, and comfort zones. While some may view change as a threat, those who embrace it see it as an opportunity to learn and evolve. Adopting this mindset requires a willingness to let go of rigid structures and expectations, allowing for fluidity and openness in the face of uncertainty.

One of the first steps in embracing change is cultivating self-awareness. By understanding your own reactions to change, you can identify patterns and triggers that influence your behavior. Reflect on past experiences of change and consider how you responded. Did you resist or adapt? What emotions arose, and how did they impact your actions? This introspection provides valuable insights into your relationship with change, allowing you to approach future transitions with greater clarity and preparedness.

Flexibility is a cornerstone of adaptability, enabling individuals to pivot and adjust when circumstances shift. Practicing flexibility involves letting go of the need for control and embracing the unknown. This can be challenging, especially for those who thrive on stability and predictability. To enhance flexibility, start by experimenting with small changes in your daily routine. Whether it's taking a new route to work, trying a different hobby, or altering your schedule, these minor adjustments can build your comfort with change, making larger transitions feel less daunting.

Embracing change also requires a growth-oriented mindset that values learning and development. Approach new situations with curiosity and a willingness to explore unfamiliar territory. Instead of viewing change as a disruption, see it as an opportunity to acquire new skills, knowledge, and perspectives. This mindset not only enhances your adaptability but also fosters resilience, as it encourages you to view challenges as stepping stones rather than roadblocks.

Building a network of support is another vital aspect of embracing change. Surround yourself with individuals who encourage and inspire you, offering guidance and perspective during times of transition. Whether it's friends, family, mentors, or colleagues, these connections provide a sense of stability and reassurance, reinforcing your ability to navigate change with confidence. Engaging with diverse communities also exposes you to new ideas and experiences, enriching your understanding of the world and enhancing your adaptability.

To effectively adapt to change, it is important to develop problem-solving skills that enable you to navigate new challenges with creativity and resourcefulness. Practice brainstorming and critical thinking to explore multiple solutions to a given problem. This approach encourages innovation and opens the door to unexpected opportunities. By honing your problem-solving abilities, you equip yourself with the tools needed to face change with confidence and competence.

Maintaining a sense of purpose and direction is crucial in times of change, providing a guiding light that anchors you amidst uncertainty. Reflect on your values, goals, and priorities, ensuring that they remain aligned with your actions and decisions. This alignment creates a sense of coherence and stability, helping you navigate change with intention and clarity. When faced with difficult choices, consider how they align with your long-term vision, allowing your purpose to guide your path.

Resilience plays a key role in embracing change, as it enables individuals to recover from setbacks and maintain focus on their goals. Cultivate resilience by practicing self-care and mindfulness, ensuring that your physical, emotional, and mental well-being are prioritized. These practices enhance your ability to manage stress and adapt to new situations with grace and composure. By building resilience, you strengthen your capacity to thrive amidst change, transforming challenges into opportunities for growth and development.

Embracing change also involves letting go of the fear of failure, recognizing that mistakes and setbacks are integral to the learning process. Approach change with a spirit of experimentation, allowing yourself the freedom to try new things without the pressure of perfection. When faced with failure, analyze the experience objectively, extracting valuable lessons and insights that inform your future actions. This perspective fosters a growth mindset, encouraging you to embrace change as a pathway to learning and innovation.

The Power of Positive Thinking

Positive thinking is a transformative force that shapes the way we perceive the world and interact with it. It is more than just a fleeting feeling of contentment; it is a mindset that can influence our emotions, decisions, and actions. By harnessing the power of positive thinking, we can enhance our well-being, improve our relationships, and unlock our potential for success and fulfillment.

At its core, positive thinking involves focusing on the good in any given situation. It means acknowledging challenges and setbacks without allowing them to overshadow the positive aspects of our lives. This mindset encourages us to approach life with optimism and resilience, fostering a sense of hope and possibility even in the face of adversity. By choosing to concentrate on positive thoughts, we can reframe our experiences and transform our outlook on life.

The impact of positive thinking extends beyond our mental and emotional states; it can also influence our physical health. Studies have shown that individuals who maintain a positive outlook tend to experience lower levels of stress and anxiety, reduced risk of chronic diseases, and improved immune function. This is because positive thinking promotes healthier coping mechanisms, enabling individuals to manage stress more effectively and maintain a balanced lifestyle.

To cultivate positive thinking, it is essential to become aware of your internal dialogue and the thoughts that shape your perception of the world. Pay attention to the language you use when reflecting on your experiences and interactions. Are your thoughts predominantly critical or supportive? Do you focus on problems or solutions? By identifying negative thought patterns, you can begin to challenge and reframe them, fostering a more positive mindset.

One effective technique for cultivating positive thinking is the practice of gratitude. Gratitude involves recognizing and appreciating the good things in our lives, no matter how small or seemingly insignificant. By regularly expressing gratitude, we shift our focus from what is lacking to what is abundant, enhancing our sense of contentment and well-being. Consider keeping a gratitude journal, in which you document three things you are grateful for each day. This simple practice can help reinforce positive thinking and create a habit of appreciation.

Visualization is another powerful tool for promoting positive thinking. By creating vivid mental images of success and happiness, we can reinforce our belief in our ability to achieve our goals and realize our dreams. Visualize yourself navigating challenges with confidence, achieving your aspirations, and experiencing joy and fulfillment. This mental rehearsal can boost your confidence and motivation, making positive outcomes feel more attainable and realistic.

Surrounding yourself with positivity is also crucial to fostering a positive mindset. Engage with individuals who inspire and uplift you, offering encouragement and support. Seek out environments and activities that bring you joy and fulfillment, whether it's spending time in nature, pursuing a creative hobby, or engaging in meaningful conversations. By immersing yourself in positive influences, you reinforce your commitment to a positive outlook and create a supportive network for growth and development.

Mindfulness and meditation can enhance positive thinking by promoting present-moment awareness and reducing stress. These practices encourage you to observe your thoughts and emotions without judgment, allowing you to respond to life's challenges with clarity and composure. By cultivating mindfulness, you can become more attuned to the positive aspects of your experiences, fostering a deeper sense of appreciation and contentment.

Setting realistic and achievable goals is an important aspect of positive thinking, as it provides a sense of direction and purpose. Break your goals into manageable steps, celebrating each accomplishment along the way. This approach not only reinforces your belief in your ability to succeed but also fosters a sense of progress and fulfillment. By focusing on achievable goals, you build momentum and motivation, propelling you toward greater success and satisfaction.

Practicing self-compassion is essential for maintaining a positive mindset, as it encourages kindness and understanding toward oneself. Acknowledge that everyone experiences setbacks and difficulties, and that these challenges do not diminish your worth or potential. By treating yourself with the same empathy and patience you would offer a friend, you create a nurturing environment for growth and resilience.

While positive thinking is a powerful tool, it is important to balance optimism with realism. This means acknowledging challenges and potential obstacles without becoming overwhelmed by them. By maintaining a realistic perspective, you can approach situations with a clear understanding of the potential risks and rewards, allowing you to make informed decisions and take calculated actions.

Chapter 4

Creating a Motivational Environment

Designing Your Ideal Workspace

Creating an ideal workspace is a vital component in optimizing productivity, creativity, and overall well-being. The environment in which we work significantly influences our focus, motivation, and efficiency. By designing a workspace that caters to our personal preferences and professional needs, we can enhance our performance and foster a sense of satisfaction and accomplishment.

The first step in designing your ideal workspace is to identify your specific needs and preferences. Consider the nature of your work and the tasks you engage in regularly. Do you require a quiet space for deep concentration, or do you thrive in a dynamic environment with background noise? Are you primarily working on a computer, or do you need space for hands-on activities and projects? Understanding these requirements will guide your decisions regarding the layout, furniture, and tools needed to support your work effectively.

Once you have a clear understanding of your needs, evaluate the physical space available to you. Whether you have a dedicated office, a corner of a room, or a shared workspace, it's essential to make the most of the area you have. Begin by decluttering and organizing the space, removing any unnecessary items that may distract or impede your workflow. A clean and organized environment can significantly enhance your mental clarity and focus, creating a foundation for productivity.

Ergonomics plays a crucial role in designing a workspace that promotes comfort and well-being. Ensure that your desk and chair are positioned at the appropriate height to support good posture and reduce strain on your body. Invest in an ergonomic chair that provides proper lumbar support, and consider using a stand for your computer monitor to keep it at eye level. These adjustments can prevent discomfort and fatigue, allowing you to work efficiently for extended periods.

Lighting is another essential element in creating an ideal workspace. Natural light is the most beneficial, as it reduces eye strain and enhances mood and productivity. Position your desk near a window if possible, allowing natural light to illuminate your workspace. If natural light is limited, invest in quality artificial lighting that mimics daylight, providing ample illumination for your tasks. Adjustable desk lamps can also offer focused lighting for specific activities, such as reading or writing.

Personalization adds a layer of comfort and inspiration to your workspace, making it a place where you feel motivated and engaged. Incorporate elements that reflect your personality and interests, such as artwork, plants, or personal mementos. These touches can create a sense of ownership and connection to your environment, boosting your mood and fostering creativity. However, be mindful not to overcrowd the space with too many personal items, as this can lead to distraction.

Technology plays a significant role in modern workspaces, and optimizing your tech setup can enhance efficiency and streamline your workflow. Ensure that your computer, software, and peripherals are up-to-date and functioning properly. Consider investing in noise-canceling headphones if you work in a shared or noisy environment, allowing you to focus on your tasks without interruption. Additionally, organize cables and wires to prevent clutter and maintain a tidy workspace.

Incorporating elements that promote well-being and relaxation can enhance the overall atmosphere of your workspace. Consider adding a small indoor plant or a diffuser with calming essential oils to create a soothing ambiance. These elements can reduce stress and increase productivity, providing a sense of tranquility amidst a busy workday. Taking regular breaks to stretch, breathe, or meditate can also contribute to a positive work environment and prevent burnout.

Flexibility is an important consideration when designing your workspace, as it allows for adaptability and creativity. Arrange your furniture and tools in a way that accommodates different working styles and activities. For instance, consider using a sit-stand desk that allows you to alternate between sitting and standing throughout the day, promoting movement and reducing fatigue. A mobile workstation or adjustable shelving can also provide versatility, enabling you to reconfigure the space as needed.

Collaboration and communication are essential aspects of many work environments, and your workspace should facilitate these interactions. Ensure that your setup includes tools for effective communication, such as video conferencing equipment or a whiteboard for brainstorming sessions. Arrange seating and furniture to accommodate meetings or group work, creating a welcoming space for collaboration and idea-sharing. By fostering a collaborative environment, you can enhance teamwork and innovation.

Lastly, regular maintenance and evaluation of your workspace are crucial to ensuring its effectiveness and functionality. Periodically assess the layout, tools, and elements of your environment to determine if they continue to meet your needs and support your goals. Make adjustments as necessary to accommodate changes in your work or personal preferences. By staying attuned to your evolving requirements, you can maintain a workspace that remains conducive to productivity and well-being.

Building a Supportive Network

In the tapestry of life, relationships are the threads that weave our experiences together, providing support, guidance, and companionship. Building a supportive network is essential for personal and professional growth, offering a foundation of trust and collaboration that empowers individuals to navigate challenges and seize opportunities. This network, comprised of friends, family, mentors, and colleagues, serves as a vital source of encouragement and wisdom, enriching our journeys with shared insights and diverse perspectives.

Cultivating a supportive network begins with identifying the key individuals in your life who uplift and inspire you. These are the people who believe in your potential, celebrate your successes, and offer a listening ear during difficult times. Reflect on the relationships you currently have and consider which ones align with these qualities. It is important to nurture these connections, investing time and energy into maintaining them and expressing gratitude for their presence in your life.

Communication is the cornerstone of any supportive relationship, fostering understanding and connection between individuals. Practice active listening, offering your full attention and empathy to those in your network. By creating a space for open and honest dialogue, you build trust and strengthen your relationships, allowing others to feel valued and heard. In turn, this encourages them to reciprocate, creating a cycle of mutual support and respect.

Mentorship is a powerful component of a supportive network, providing guidance and insight from those with more experience or expertise. Seek out mentors who can offer valuable perspectives on your personal or professional goals, helping you navigate challenges and make informed decisions. Be proactive in building these relationships, reaching out with genuine curiosity and a willingness to learn. In return, consider offering mentorship to others, sharing your own experiences and knowledge to support their growth and development.

Diversity is an important aspect of a supportive network, as it enriches your understanding of the world and broadens your perspective. Engage with individuals from different backgrounds, cultures, and experiences, embracing the opportunity to learn from their unique insights. This diversity not only enhances your personal growth but also fosters innovation and creativity, as it encourages you to approach problems and opportunities from multiple angles.

In the digital age, technology offers a wealth of tools for building and maintaining a supportive network. Social media platforms, professional networks, and online communities provide avenues for connecting with others who share your interests and goals. Leverage these resources to expand your network, engaging with individuals who inspire and challenge you. However, be mindful of the quality of these connections, prioritizing meaningful interactions over quantity.

Collaboration is a key element of a supportive network, as it enables individuals to pool their talents and resources to achieve common goals. Seek out opportunities for collaboration, whether through joint projects, brainstorming sessions, or shared initiatives. By working together, you can leverage each other's strengths and expertise, creating outcomes that are greater than the sum of their parts. Collaboration also fosters a sense of camaraderie and shared purpose, reinforcing the bonds within your network.

Boundaries are an essential consideration when building a supportive network, as they ensure that relationships remain healthy and respectful. Establish clear boundaries that protect your time, energy, and well-being, communicating them openly with those in your network. By setting and respecting boundaries, you create a foundation of trust and mutual respect, allowing relationships to flourish without becoming overwhelming or draining.

Reciprocity is a fundamental principle of a supportive network, emphasizing the importance of giving as well as receiving. Offer your support and assistance to others, whether through acts of kindness, sharing resources, or providing encouragement. By contributing to the well-being of those in your network, you reinforce the bonds of connection and create a culture of generosity and collaboration. This reciprocity not only strengthens relationships but also enhances your own sense of fulfillment and purpose.

Adaptability is crucial in maintaining a supportive network, as relationships evolve and change over time. Be open to the natural ebb and flow of connections, recognizing that some relationships may deepen while others may fade. Embrace these changes with grace and flexibility, allowing your network to grow and adapt alongside you. By remaining open to new connections and experiences, you ensure that your network remains dynamic and relevant to your evolving needs and aspirations.

The Impact of Surroundings on Motivation

The environment we inhabit exerts a profound influence on our motivation and productivity. Our surroundings subtly shape our thoughts, emotions, and actions, often without us realizing it. By understanding the impact of our environment on our motivation, we can make intentional choices to create spaces that invigorate and inspire us, propelling us towards our goals with renewed energy and focus.

Consider the story of Emma, a freelance graphic designer who found herself struggling with creativity and motivation. Her workspace was cluttered, dimly lit, and uninspiring. It wasn't until she decided to revamp her environment that she noticed a remarkable difference. By decluttering her desk, introducing natural light, and adding elements of personal significance, Emma transformed her surroundings into a haven of creativity. This change not only reignited her motivation but also enhanced her productivity and satisfaction with her work.

The physical aspects of our environment, such as lighting, color, and layout, play a crucial role in influencing our motivation. Natural light, for instance, has been shown to boost mood and energy levels, making it a vital component of an inspiring workspace. Positioning your desk near a window or using daylight-mimicking bulbs can enhance your mental clarity and focus, creating a more invigorating atmosphere. In contrast, dim or harsh lighting can lead to eye strain and fatigue, diminishing motivation and productivity.

Color psychology also offers valuable insights into the impact of surroundings on motivation. Different colors evoke distinct emotions and responses, influencing our mood and behavior. For example, blue is often associated with calmness and concentration, making it an ideal choice for spaces where focus is required. Green, linked to nature and balance, can promote a sense of tranquility and well-being. Meanwhile, vibrant colors like red and orange can stimulate energy and creativity, making them suitable for areas dedicated to brainstorming and innovation. By deliberately choosing colors that align with your goals and tasks, you can create an environment that enhances your motivation and performance.

The layout and organization of your space can significantly affect your motivation and efficiency. A cluttered and disorganized environment can lead to feelings of overwhelm and distraction, sapping your energy and focus. In contrast, a tidy and organized space fosters a sense of control and clarity, enabling you to concentrate on your tasks with greater ease. Consider implementing systems for organization, such as designated storage areas, filing systems, or digital tools, to maintain a clutter-free environment that supports your motivation.

Personalization is another powerful factor in creating a motivating environment. Incorporating elements that reflect your personality and interests can infuse your space with meaning and inspiration. Whether it's artwork, plants, or memorabilia, these personal touches can evoke positive emotions and reinforce your connection to your environment. For Emma, adding plants and inspirational quotes to her workspace created a sense of vibrancy and purpose, reminding her of her passion for design and her commitment to her craft.

The impact of your surroundings extends beyond the physical realm, encompassing the social and cultural environment as well. The people you interact with and the culture of your workplace or community can influence your motivation and drive. Surrounding yourself with supportive and like-minded individuals can foster a sense of camaraderie and encouragement, motivating you to pursue your goals with enthusiasm. Conversely, a toxic or unsupportive environment can drain your energy and hinder your progress.

To cultivate a motivating social environment, seek out connections with individuals who share your values and aspirations. Engage in communities or groups that inspire and challenge you, offering opportunities for collaboration and growth. This sense of belonging and shared purpose can enhance your motivation and commitment, creating a network of support that propels you towards success.

Creating an environment that nurtures motivation also involves setting boundaries and managing distractions. In today's digital age, distractions are abundant, often pulling us away from our priorities and goals. Establishing boundaries, such as designated work hours, device-free zones, or scheduled breaks, can help you maintain focus and productivity. By minimizing distractions and protecting your time and energy, you create a space that supports your motivation and enables you to achieve your objectives.

The impact of surroundings on motivation is an intricate interplay of physical, social, and psychological factors. By intentionally shaping your environment to align with your goals and values, you can create a space that energizes and inspires you.

Whether it's through adjusting lighting, choosing colors, organizing your space, or fostering supportive relationships, these deliberate choices can enhance your motivation and propel you towards success.

Leveraging Technology for Inspiration

Technology, in its myriad forms, has woven itself into the tapestry of our daily lives, offering tools and platforms that can spark creativity and fuel inspiration. The digital age has transformed the way we access information, communicate ideas, and express ourselves, providing endless opportunities to explore new horizons. By leveraging technology, we can tap into a wellspring of inspiration that enhances our personal and professional endeavors.

The internet is a vast repository of knowledge and creativity, serving as a gateway to inspiration from around the world. With a few clicks, you can access a wealth of resources, from online courses and tutorials to forums and communities where ideas are shared and cultivated. This accessibility allows you to explore new interests, acquire new skills, and connect with individuals who share your passions. Whether you're interested in learning a new language, honing your artistic abilities, or exploring scientific advancements, the internet provides a platform for growth and discovery.

Social media platforms have revolutionized the way we share and consume content, offering a visual and interactive medium for inspiration. Platforms like Instagram, Pinterest, and YouTube showcase a myriad of creative works, from art and photography to design and innovation. By curating your feeds to include content that resonates with you, you can immerse yourself in a world of inspiration that fuels your creativity and broadens your perspective. Engaging with creators and communities on these platforms can also foster collaboration and idea exchange, enriching your creative journey.

Digital tools and software offer powerful capabilities for expressing and realizing creative ideas. From graphic design and video editing software to music production and writing applications, technology provides the means to bring your visions to life. Experimenting with these tools can unlock new dimensions of creativity, enabling you to explore different mediums and techniques. For instance, a writer might experiment with storytelling through multimedia, while an artist might explore digital painting techniques. These tools not only enhance your creative abilities but also offer opportunities for innovation and experimentation.

Virtual and augmented reality technologies are pushing the boundaries of inspiration, offering immersive experiences that transport us to new worlds and perspectives. These technologies enable us to explore environments and narratives in ways that were previously unimaginable, opening up new avenues for creative expression. Whether it's experiencing a virtual art gallery, participating in an interactive storytelling experience, or exploring a simulated environment, virtual and augmented reality can ignite the imagination and inspire fresh ideas.

Collaboration platforms and communication tools have transformed the way we work and create together, breaking down geographical barriers and fostering global connections. Tools like Slack, Zoom, and Trello facilitate seamless collaboration, allowing individuals and teams to work together in real-time, regardless of location. This connectivity enables the exchange of ideas and expertise, fostering a culture of innovation and creativity. By collaborating with others, you can gain new insights and perspectives, enriching your creative process and inspiring new possibilities.

While technology offers vast potential for inspiration, it's important to approach it with intention and mindfulness. The digital world can be overwhelming, with an abundance of content and information vying for our attention. To leverage technology effectively, it's crucial to set boundaries and prioritize the quality of your engagement. Curate your digital experience by selecting platforms and content that align with your interests and goals, and be mindful of screen time to prevent burnout and fatigue.

Balancing digital and analog experiences can also enhance your creative process and inspiration. While technology offers powerful tools and resources, stepping away from screens and engaging with the physical world can provide a fresh perspective and rejuvenate your creativity. Whether it's taking a walk in nature, sketching in a notebook, or engaging in hands-on activities, these analog experiences can stimulate your senses and inspire new ideas. By blending digital and analog approaches, you create a holistic environment for creativity and inspiration.

Incorporating technology into your creative routine requires adaptability and a willingness to explore new possibilities. Embrace the learning curve that comes with mastering new tools and platforms, and experiment with different approaches to find what resonates with you. This adaptability not only enhances your creative abilities but also fosters a growth mindset, encouraging you to view challenges as opportunities for learning and innovation.

As you navigate the digital landscape, consider the ethical implications of your engagement with technology. Be mindful of the sources and content you consume, and strive to support creators and communities that align with your values. Practice digital citizenship by engaging respectfully and responsibly, contributing positively to the online communities you are part of. By approaching technology with integrity and purpose, you can create an environment that supports both your inspiration and the well-being of others.

Balancing Work and Relaxation

Finding the right balance between work and relaxation is a delicate dance that many strive to perfect. It's a crucial aspect of living a fulfilling and healthy life, yet it often eludes those caught in the hustle and bustle of modern existence. The demands of work, coupled with the constant connectivity of technology, can make it challenging to carve out time for rest and rejuvenation. However, achieving this balance is not only possible but essential for overall well-being and productivity.

Consider the story of Jack, a dedicated professional who found himself perpetually tethered to his work. Emails, meetings, and deadlines occupied his days, leaving little room for relaxation or personal time. Over time, the relentless pace took a toll on Jack's health and happiness. It wasn't until he consciously decided to address this imbalance that he began to see improvements in his life. By implementing strategies to separate work from leisure, Jack discovered a renewed sense of energy and focus, enhancing both his professional performance and personal fulfillment.

One of the key strategies in balancing work and relaxation is establishing clear boundaries. In a world where work can easily spill over into personal time, setting defined limits is crucial. Designate specific work hours and adhere to them, creating a routine that respects both professional and personal commitments. Communicate these boundaries to colleagues and clients, setting expectations for when you are available and when you are not. This clarity not only safeguards your time but also fosters a culture of respect and understanding in your work environment.

Prioritization is another important aspect of maintaining balance. With a myriad of tasks and responsibilities vying for attention, it's essential to identify what truly matters and allocate time accordingly. Use tools like to-do lists or digital planners to organize tasks by urgency and importance, ensuring that critical obligations are addressed while leaving room for breaks and downtime. By focusing on what is most important, you can avoid the trap of constant busyness and create space for relaxation and renewal.

Incorporating regular breaks into your workday can significantly enhance your ability to balance work with relaxation. Short, frequent breaks have been shown to improve focus and productivity, preventing burnout and fatigue. Whether it's a five-minute stretch, a walk around the block, or a moment of mindfulness, these pauses provide an opportunity to recharge and reset. Consider using techniques like the Pomodoro Technique, which involves working in focused intervals followed by short breaks, to structure your time effectively.

Creating a dedicated space for relaxation is also vital in establishing a balance. Just as you have a workspace for professional tasks, designate an area in your home or environment where you can unwind and disconnect. This space should be free from work-related distractions, offering a sanctuary for rest and leisure. Fill this area with elements that promote relaxation, such as comfortable seating, calming colors, or soothing music. By creating a physical boundary between work and relaxation, you can more easily transition between the two, fostering a sense of balance and harmony.

Mindfulness and self-awareness are powerful tools in achieving balance. Cultivate a practice of checking in with yourself, assessing your energy levels, emotions, and needs. This self-reflection can guide you in making informed decisions about when to push forward and when to step back. Mindfulness practices, such as meditation or deep breathing exercises, can also help center your thoughts and promote relaxation, providing a valuable counterbalance to the demands of work.

It's important to recognize that relaxation doesn't always mean doing nothing. Engaging in activities that bring joy and fulfillment can be a form of relaxation, offering a sense of purpose and satisfaction. Whether it's pursuing a hobby, spending time with loved ones, or exploring nature, these activities provide an opportunity to recharge and reconnect with yourself and others. By making time for the things you love, you enrich your life and create a more holistic balance between work and relaxation.

The role of technology in balancing work and relaxation cannot be overlooked. While technology offers incredible tools for productivity and connectivity, it can also blur the lines between work and personal time. Be mindful of how and when you use technology, setting limits on screen time and disconnecting from devices during relaxation periods. Consider using apps or settings that help manage notifications and prioritize time away from screens, allowing you to be fully present in moments of rest.

Flexibility is an essential component of maintaining balance, as life's demands and circumstances can change unexpectedly. Be open to adjusting your approach to work and relaxation as needed, allowing for fluidity in your routines and priorities. This adaptability enables you to respond to challenges with resilience, maintaining a sense of equilibrium even in the face of change.

Ultimately, balancing work and relaxation is an ongoing process that requires intention and commitment. It's about creating a lifestyle that honors both your professional aspirations and personal well-being, allowing you to thrive in all aspects of life. By establishing boundaries, prioritizing tasks, and incorporating relaxation into your routine, you can cultivate a sense of balance that supports your goals and nurtures your spirit.

Chapter 5

Strategies for Sustaining Motivation

Breaking Goals into Achievable Steps

Setting goals is an essential part of personal and professional growth, yet the journey from aspiration to achievement can often feel daunting. The key to transforming ambitious dreams into reality lies in the art of breaking goals into manageable, achievable steps. By deconstructing larger objectives into smaller tasks, you can create a clear roadmap for success, enabling you to navigate challenges with confidence and purpose.

Imagine Sarah, an aspiring author with a vision of publishing her first novel. The prospect of writing an entire book seemed overwhelming, leaving her paralyzed by the enormity of the task. It wasn't until Sarah began to break down her goal into smaller, actionable steps that she found the clarity and motivation she needed. By setting daily word count targets, planning her story structure, and dedicating specific time slots for writing, Sarah gradually made progress, transforming her dream into a tangible reality.

The first step in breaking goals into achievable components is to clearly define your overarching objective. Take the time to articulate what you want to achieve, ensuring that the goal is specific, measurable, attainable, relevant, and time-bound (SMART). This clarity provides a foundation for developing a structured plan, allowing you to focus your efforts and resources effectively.

Once you have a well-defined goal, begin the process of deconstruction by identifying the key milestones or phases required to achieve it. These milestones serve as intermediate checkpoints, marking significant progress along the way. For Sarah, these milestones included completing the outline, drafting each chapter, and revising the manuscript. By segmenting the goal into phases, you create a sense of direction and momentum, motivating you to keep moving forward.

With the milestones in place, delve deeper by breaking them down into smaller, actionable tasks. These tasks should be specific and manageable, enabling you to make consistent progress without feeling overwhelmed. Consider using techniques such as task lists or project management tools to organize and prioritize these tasks, ensuring that each step builds upon the previous one. For instance, Sarah's tasks included researching character backgrounds, writing daily for a set period, and seeking feedback from peers. By focusing on these smaller tasks, you can maintain a sense of accomplishment and motivation throughout the journey.

Time management plays a crucial role in achieving your goals, and it is essential to allocate dedicated time for each task. Establish a realistic timeline, taking into account your existing commitments and responsibilities. Consider creating a schedule or calendar that outlines when each task will be completed, allowing you to track progress and adjust as needed. For Sarah, setting aside specific hours each day for writing helped her maintain consistency and discipline, transforming her goal into a daily habit.

Accountability is another powerful tool in the pursuit of your goals. Sharing your objectives with a trusted friend, mentor, or accountability partner can provide valuable support and encouragement. Regular check-ins and progress updates can keep you motivated and focused, while also offering an opportunity to celebrate achievements along the way. For Sarah, discussing her progress with a writing group provided motivation and constructive feedback, helping her stay on track and overcome obstacles.

Flexibility and adaptability are essential qualities when working towards your goals. Life is unpredictable, and circumstances may require you to adjust your plans or timelines. Embrace these changes with an open mind, allowing yourself the freedom to pivot and explore new approaches. This adaptability not only enhances your resilience but also fosters a growth mindset, enabling you to learn from setbacks and continue moving forward.

As you make progress, take time to reflect on your journey and celebrate your accomplishments. Recognizing and rewarding your achievements, no matter how small, reinforces positive behavior and boosts motivation. Whether it's treating yourself to a favorite activity, sharing your success with others, or simply acknowledging your efforts, these celebrations serve as powerful reminders of your capabilities and determination.

Visualization is a technique that can enhance your ability to break goals into achievable steps. By vividly imagining the end result and the process of achieving it, you can create a mental blueprint that guides your actions and decisions. Visualization helps you internalize your goals, making them feel more attainable and real. For Sarah, envisioning her completed novel and the impact it would have on readers fueled her motivation and commitment to the writing process.

Incorporating feedback and learning from others can also enhance your progress. Seek out mentors, peers, or experts who can offer guidance, insights, and constructive criticism. By learning from their experiences and perspectives, you can refine your approach and improve your chances of success. For Sarah, engaging with other authors and participating in writing workshops provided valuable knowledge and inspiration, enriching her journey towards publication.

Ultimately, breaking goals into achievable steps is a dynamic process that requires intention, planning, and perseverance. It's about creating a path that aligns with your values and aspirations, allowing you to navigate the complexities of life with confidence and clarity. By deconstructing your goals into manageable tasks, you empower yourself to take consistent action, transforming dreams into reality one step at a time.

Celebrating Small Wins

Celebrating small wins is an essential practice in the journey of personal and professional growth. These moments of success, however minor they may seem, serve as powerful motivators and reminders of progress. By recognizing and celebrating these achievements, individuals can maintain momentum, build confidence, and foster a positive mindset that propels them toward larger goals.

Take the story of Alex, a young entrepreneur navigating the challenges of launching a startup. The road was fraught with obstacles, from securing funding to building a customer base. In the midst of the hustle, Alex learned the importance of acknowledging and celebrating each milestone, however modest. Whether it was landing the first client, receiving positive feedback, or reaching a monthly sales target, these small wins became the building blocks of confidence and motivation, sustaining Alex's drive and determination.

The concept of celebrating small wins is rooted in the psychology of motivation. Achieving a goal, no matter how small, triggers the release of dopamine, a neurotransmitter associated with pleasure and reward. This chemical response not only boosts mood but also reinforces the behavior that led to the success, encouraging individuals to continue pursuing their objectives. By intentionally celebrating these moments, individuals can leverage this natural reward system to maintain focus and enthusiasm.

One effective way to celebrate small wins is through reflection and gratitude. Taking time to acknowledge and appreciate the effort and progress made can amplify the sense of accomplishment and satisfaction. Consider keeping a journal or log where you record your achievements, big or small. This practice not only provides a tangible record of progress but also offers an opportunity for introspection and gratitude. Reflecting on these moments can help you recognize patterns of success, identify strengths, and gain insights into what drives your motivation.

Sharing your successes with others can also enhance the celebration of small wins. Whether it's with a friend, family member, or colleague, discussing your achievements can provide a sense of connection and validation. This social acknowledgment can reinforce the significance of the win, while also fostering a supportive network of encouragement. For Alex, sharing milestones with the startup team not only strengthened camaraderie but also created a culture of recognition and positivity within the company.

Incorporating rituals or rewards can add an element of fun and anticipation to the celebration of small wins. These rituals need not be extravagant; they can be simple gestures that bring joy and satisfaction. Whether it's treating yourself to a favorite meal, taking a day off to relax, or enjoying a hobby, these rewards provide a tangible representation of success. They also serve as a reminder that progress is made up of incremental achievements, each deserving of recognition.

Visualizing your progress can be a powerful motivator, reinforcing the significance of small wins. Creating a visual representation of your achievements, such as a progress chart or vision board, can provide a constant reminder of how far you've come. For Alex, a progress chart displayed in the office served as a daily source of inspiration, highlighting the cumulative impact of each milestone. This visualization not only motivated the team but also instilled a sense of pride and accomplishment.

Adopting a growth mindset is essential in embracing and celebrating small wins. This mindset, championed by psychologist Carol Dweck, emphasizes the value of effort, learning, and resilience in the pursuit of success. By viewing each win as an opportunity for growth and learning, individuals can cultivate a positive attitude towards challenges and setbacks. This perspective encourages the celebration of progress, recognizing that every step forward, no matter how small, contributes to personal and professional development.

In the pursuit of larger goals, it's easy to overlook the significance of small wins. However, these moments of success are the foundation upon which greater achievements are built. By celebrating them, individuals can boost morale, maintain motivation, and sustain momentum. For Alex, acknowledging each milestone in the startup journey not only fueled personal drive but also inspired the team to continue pushing boundaries and striving for excellence.

It's important to remember that the celebration of small wins is a personal practice, unique to each individual's preferences and values. What brings joy and satisfaction to one person may differ for another. The key is to find what resonates with you and aligns with your goals and aspirations. By making celebration an integral part of your routine, you can create a positive feedback loop that reinforces motivation and fosters a sense of fulfillment.

Maintaining Focus and Avoiding Burnout

The modern world is a whirlwind of distractions and demands, making it all too easy to lose focus and succumb to burnout. Balancing personal aspirations with professional responsibilities can leave one feeling stretched thin, constantly juggling tasks and struggling to maintain clarity. Yet, finding ways to stay focused and avoid burnout is essential for long-term success and well-being. It requires a combination of strategic planning, self-awareness, and a commitment to personal health.

Let's consider the experience of Lisa, a project manager at a bustling tech company. Lisa was known for her dedication and ability to handle multiple projects simultaneously. However, as demands increased, she found herself working longer hours, often at the expense of her personal life. The relentless pace began to erode her enthusiasm and energy, leading to fatigue and diminishing returns on her efforts. Recognizing the need for change, Lisa embarked on a journey to reclaim her focus and prevent burnout, implementing strategies that transformed her approach to work and life.

One of the most effective ways to maintain focus is to establish a clear set of priorities. With endless tasks and responsibilities, it's crucial to determine what truly matters and allocate time and resources accordingly. Begin by identifying your core objectives, both short-term and long-term, and organize tasks based on their importance and urgency. This prioritization not only helps streamline efforts but also provides a roadmap for decision-making, allowing you to focus on what truly contributes to your goals. For Lisa, creating a visual priority matrix helped her assess tasks at a glance, ensuring that her energy was directed towards meaningful outcomes.

Another key element in maintaining focus is setting boundaries. In an era of constant connectivity, it's easy for work to spill into personal time, leading to blurred lines and diminished focus. Establishing boundaries, such as designated work hours or device-free zones, helps create a separation between professional and personal life. This intentional division allows for dedicated time to recharge and refocus, fostering a sense of balance and clarity. Lisa found that setting an end time for her workday and committing to unplugging from digital devices in the evening drastically improved her mental clarity and overall well-being.

Practicing mindfulness is a powerful tool for enhancing focus and avoiding burnout. Mindfulness involves being present and fully engaged in the current moment, free from distractions and judgment. Incorporate mindfulness techniques into your daily routine, such as deep breathing exercises, meditation, or simply taking a few moments to pause and reflect. These practices help cultivate a sense of calm and clarity, enabling you to approach tasks with renewed focus and intention. For Lisa, dedicating just ten minutes each morning to mindfulness meditation set a positive tone for the day, improving her concentration and resilience.

Physical health is intrinsically linked to mental focus and energy levels. Prioritizing regular exercise, a balanced diet, and sufficient sleep are fundamental to maintaining both physical and mental well-being.

Exercise, in particular, has been shown to enhance cognitive function and reduce stress, making it an essential component of focus and productivity. By incorporating regular physical activity into her routine, Lisa experienced increased energy and improved concentration, enabling her to tackle tasks with greater efficiency.

Structured breaks are another essential aspect of maintaining focus and preventing burnout. The human brain is not designed for prolonged periods of concentration without rest. Implementing short, frequent breaks throughout the day can improve focus, creativity, and overall productivity. Techniques such as the Pomodoro Technique, which involves working in focused intervals followed by brief breaks, can help optimize concentration and energy levels. Lisa adopted this approach, finding that scheduled breaks not only enhanced her focus but also provided valuable opportunities for reflection and idea generation.

Cultivating a supportive environment is crucial in maintaining focus and avoiding burnout. Surround yourself with individuals who offer encouragement, understanding, and constructive feedback. Whether it's colleagues, friends, or mentors, a supportive network provides both motivation and perspective, helping you navigate challenges with resilience. Lisa found that engaging with a professional mentor offered valuable insights and guidance, empowering her to make informed decisions and maintain focus on her long-term goals.

Flexibility and adaptability are important qualities in managing focus and burnout. Life is unpredictable, and plans may need to adjust based on changing circumstances. Embrace these changes with an open mind, allowing yourself the freedom to pivot and explore new approaches when necessary. This adaptability not only enhances resilience but also encourages continuous learning and growth. For Lisa, adopting a flexible mindset allowed her to view challenges as opportunities for innovation and creativity, maintaining motivation and focus even in the face of uncertainty.

Recognizing the signs of burnout is essential for addressing it before it becomes overwhelming. Symptoms such as chronic fatigue, irritability, and a sense of detachment are indicators that it's time to reassess your approach to work and life. By being attuned to these signals, you can take proactive steps to restore balance and protect your well-being. Lisa learned to recognize these signs and respond by prioritizing self-care and seeking support, ensuring that her health and focus remained a top priority.

Ultimately, maintaining focus and avoiding burnout is an ongoing journey that requires intentionality and self-awareness. It's about creating a lifestyle that honors both your ambitions and well-being, allowing you to thrive personally and professionally. By establishing priorities, setting boundaries, and incorporating mindfulness and self-care practices, you can cultivate a sustainable approach to focus and productivity, achieving your goals with clarity and energy.

The Art of Prioritization

Prioritization is an art form that, when mastered, can transform chaos into clarity and overwhelm into manageable tasks. In a world brimming with distractions and competing demands, the ability to discern what truly matters and act accordingly is a skill that can significantly enhance productivity and satisfaction. The art of prioritization involves not just making lists, but understanding the nuances of urgency, importance, and the impact of each task on your broader goals.

Consider the case of Tom, a marketing executive at a fast-paced agency. Every day, Tom was bombarded with emails, meetings, and project deadlines, each clamoring for his immediate attention. The sheer volume of tasks often left him feeling scattered and stressed. However, by learning to prioritize effectively, Tom was able to streamline his workload, focusing on tasks that delivered the most value and aligning his efforts with the agency's strategic objectives.

The foundation of effective prioritization lies in understanding the difference between urgency and importance. Urgency refers to tasks that require immediate attention, often driven by deadlines or external pressures. Importance, on the other hand, relates to tasks that contribute to long-term goals and objectives. The challenge is to balance these two dimensions, ensuring that urgent tasks do not overshadow those that are important for sustained success. Using a prioritization matrix, such as the Eisenhower Box, can help categorize tasks based on these criteria, allowing you to focus on what truly matters.

Once tasks are categorized, the next step is to evaluate their impact. Not all tasks carry the same weight or significance, and understanding the potential outcomes of each can guide decision-making. Consider the potential benefits, risks, and opportunities associated with each task, and prioritize those that offer the greatest return on investment. For Tom, this meant prioritizing client presentations and strategic planning over administrative tasks, ensuring that his efforts aligned with the agency's growth objectives.

Time management is a critical component of prioritization. Allocating time effectively involves not just scheduling tasks, but creating a structured routine that accommodates both focused work and necessary breaks. Establishing time blocks for specific activities can help manage distractions and maintain concentration. Tom implemented a daily routine that included dedicated blocks for creative work, client meetings, and strategic planning, allowing him to allocate his mental energy efficiently.

Flexibility is an essential aspect of prioritization, as priorities may shift based on changing circumstances or new information. Being adaptable and open to reevaluating priorities ensures that your approach remains relevant and effective. Regularly reviewing and adjusting priorities can help you stay aligned with evolving goals and respond proactively to challenges. For Tom, weekly reviews of his priorities allowed him to make informed adjustments, keeping his efforts in sync with the agency's dynamic environment.

Delegation is another powerful tool in the art of prioritization. Recognizing that you cannot do everything alone and entrusting tasks to others can free up valuable time for high-impact activities. Effective delegation involves identifying tasks that can be handled by others, selecting the right individuals for the job, and providing clear instructions and expectations. By delegating routine tasks to his team, Tom was able to focus on strategic initiatives, leveraging his expertise where it mattered most.

Technology can also aid in prioritization, offering tools and platforms that enhance organization and efficiency. Task management software, digital calendars, and collaboration platforms provide a centralized space for tracking tasks, setting deadlines, and collaborating with others. These tools can streamline workflows and ensure that priorities are visible and accessible. Tom utilized project management software to organize his tasks and monitor progress, allowing for seamless coordination with his team.

Self-awareness and reflection are vital components of effective prioritization. Understanding your strengths, weaknesses, and work preferences can help you tailor your approach to prioritization. Reflect on past experiences and identify patterns or habits that have influenced your ability to prioritize effectively. By recognizing these patterns, you can make informed adjustments and develop strategies that enhance your prioritization skills. Tom found that reflecting on his daily accomplishments and challenges provided valuable insights, informing his future decisions and actions.

Emotional intelligence plays a role in prioritization, as emotions can influence decision-making and task management. Being aware of your emotional state and how it affects your priorities can help you make more rational and objective decisions. Practice techniques such as mindfulness or journaling to manage stress and maintain focus, ensuring that emotions do not cloud judgment. For Tom, incorporating mindfulness practices into his routine helped him maintain composure and clarity, even in high-pressure situations.

Ultimately, the art of prioritization is about creating a balance between immediate demands and long-term aspirations, allowing you to navigate the complexities of modern life with intention and purpose. By understanding the nuances of urgency and importance, evaluating the impact of tasks, and leveraging tools and techniques, you can enhance your ability to prioritize effectively, achieving both personal and professional success.

Cultivating Patience and Persistence

Cultivating patience and persistence is essential for anyone aiming to succeed in a world that often demands immediate results. These qualities are not just virtues but vital skills that empower individuals to navigate challenges, setbacks, and the unpredictable nature of life's journey. By embracing patience and persistence, one can sustain motivation and achieve long-term goals, even when the path is fraught with obstacles.

Consider the story of Mia, an aspiring musician with dreams of performing on the world stage. Her journey was not a straightforward ascent to fame but a series of trials and tribulations that tested her resolve and dedication. Mia faced numerous rejections from record labels, struggled with self-doubt, and encountered financial difficulties. However, her unwavering patience and relentless persistence fueled her determination to continue honing her craft, eventually leading to her breakthrough moment. Mia's story exemplifies the power of these qualities in transforming aspirations into reality.

Patience is more than just waiting for results; it is an active state of endurance that involves maintaining a positive attitude and a clear vision. It requires a shift in perspective, viewing delays and setbacks as opportunities for growth rather than as barriers to success. By adopting this mindset, individuals can manage expectations and reduce the frustration associated with slow progress. For Mia, patience meant accepting that her musical journey would take time and embracing each step as a learning experience.

One practical approach to cultivating patience is to set realistic and achievable goals. By breaking down larger objectives into smaller, manageable tasks, individuals can focus on incremental progress rather than becoming overwhelmed by the end goal. This approach not only makes the journey more manageable but also provides regular opportunities for celebration and reflection. Mia set daily practice goals and performance targets, allowing her to track her progress and stay motivated.

Mindfulness and meditation are valuable tools for developing patience. These practices encourage presence and awareness, helping individuals stay grounded and centered even in the face of delays or setbacks. Mindfulness can enhance emotional regulation, enabling individuals to respond to challenges with calmness and composure. Mia incorporated mindfulness into her daily routine, using it to manage stress and maintain focus during auditions and performances.

Persistence, on the other hand, is the unyielding determination to continue striving toward goals despite difficulties or opposition. It involves resilience and adaptability, the ability to bounce back from failures and adjust strategies as needed. Persistence requires a proactive approach, seeking solutions and alternatives when faced with obstacles. For Mia, persistence meant continuously refining her skills, seeking feedback, and exploring new avenues for her music.

Building a support network is crucial for sustaining persistence. Surrounding oneself with mentors, peers, and allies who offer encouragement and constructive feedback can bolster motivation and resilience. This support system provides reassurance and perspective, reminding individuals that they are not alone in their journey. Mia found strength in her community of fellow musicians, who offered guidance and inspiration during challenging times.

Self-compassion is a vital component of both patience and persistence. Being kind to oneself and acknowledging that setbacks are a natural part of the process can alleviate the pressure of perfectionism and reduce self-criticism. Self-compassion fosters a growth mindset, encouraging individuals to view failures as opportunities for learning and improvement. Mia practiced self-compassion by celebrating her efforts, regardless of the outcome, and recognizing that each setback was a step toward growth.

Developing a growth mindset is essential for cultivating patience and persistence. This mindset, characterized by the belief that abilities and intelligence can be developed through effort and learning, empowers individuals to embrace challenges and persevere in the face of adversity. By focusing on progress rather than perfection, individuals can maintain motivation and resilience.

Mia adopted a growth mindset, viewing each performance as a chance to learn and grow, rather than as a final judgment of her abilities.

Visualization is another powerful technique for fostering patience and persistence. By vividly imagining the journey toward a goal, individuals can create a mental roadmap that guides their actions and decisions. Visualization helps reinforce commitment and motivation, providing a clear picture of the desired outcome. Mia used visualization to imagine her performances and the impact of her music, fueling her determination to persist despite challenges.

Celebrating small wins is integral to maintaining patience and persistence. Recognizing and appreciating incremental achievements provides a sense of accomplishment and motivation, reinforcing the value of sustained effort. These celebrations serve as reminders of progress and the importance of perseverance. Mia celebrated each successful performance and positive feedback, using these moments to bolster her confidence and commitment.

Ultimately, cultivating patience and persistence is an ongoing journey that requires intention and practice. It's about embracing the process and recognizing that success is not a destination but a continuous path of growth and discovery. By nurturing these qualities, individuals can navigate the complexities of life with resilience and determination, transforming challenges into opportunities for personal and professional development.